War and Peace in Kurdistan

Perspectives for a Political Solution of the Kurdish Question

By Abdullah Öcalan

Published by International Initiative
"Freedom for Abdullah Öcalan – Peace in Kurdistan"
Cologne 2012
Produced by Transmedia Publishing
ISBN 978-3-942961059

Inhalt

1. Foreword

Life in the Middle East is characterized and determined by numerous conflicts, many of which may appear rather strange to western eyes and incompatible with western ideas and western concepts of ratio and logos. This impression is also true of the Kurdish question, a term that describes one of the most complex and bloody fields of conflict in the Middle East yet unresolved. However, as long as we do not discuss all dimensions of this conflict equally, it will continue and even further aggravate, thus creating new far-reaching problems. The historical, economical and political dimensions of the Kurdish question exceed by far the Arab-Israeli conflict, which, in contrast to the Kurdish question, enjoys the attention of the international public. Knowledge about this conflict is limited, and because it is taking place in one of the most central regions of the Middle East both with respect to demography and geostrategic importance, this deficit often results in one-sided and superficial analysis of this complex problem.

Since the settlement area of the Kurds spans the present territories of Arabs, Persians, and Turks the Kurdish question necessarily influences most of the region. A solution in one part of Kurdistan also affects other parts of Kurdistan and neighboring countries. Conversely, the destructive approach of actors in one country may have negative effects for the solution of the Kurdish question in one of the other countries. The rugged Kurdish landscape is practically made for armed struggle, and the Kurds have been fighting colonization or conquest by foreign powers since time immemorial. Resistance has become part of their life and culture.

At the beginning of solution process, the conflict needs to be recognized and defined. With a view to the Kurdish question, a realistic definition of the Kurdish phenomenon is therefore important. However, it is here already, where much of the disagreement begins. While the Arabs call the Kurds "Arabs from Yemen" the Turks call them "mountain Turks and the Persians regard them as their ethnic counterparts. It is not astonishing, therefore, that their political stance in the Kurdish question is marked by arguments over definitions.

The Kurdish question has emerged out of the blue. It is the product of a long historical process and does not have much in common with similar issues in other parts of the world. In fact, there are some fundamental peculiarities and differences. Either of them needs to be defined in a solution process. Any policy building merely on apparent common ground leads to irresolvable problems. A policy targeted on a solution needs to realistically analyze the phenomenon and include both the national, political and social background and also all parties involved in the conflict. It is indispensable, therefore, to recognize the existence of the Kurdish phenomenon. This, on the other hand, is not possible without information about the historical background.

2. Etymology of the Words Kurd and Kurdistan

The name Kurdistan goes back to the Sumerian word Kur, which meant something like mountain more than 5,000 years ago. The suffix ti stood for being related to something. The word kurti then had the meaning of mountain tribe or mountain people. The Luwians, a people settling in western Anatolia about 3,000 years ago called Kurdistan Gondwana, which meant land of the villages in their language. In Kurdish, gond is until today the word for village. During the reign of Assure the Kurds were called Nairi, which meant as much as people by the river.

In the middle ages under the reign of the Arab sultanates, the Kurdish areas were referred to as Beled-Ekrat. The Seljuk Sultans who spoke Persian were the first who used the word Kurdistan, land of the Kurds, in their official communiqués. The ottoman sultans also called the settlement area of the Kurds Kurdistan. Until the twenties of the last century, this was a generally used name. After 1925, the existence of the Kurds was denied, particularly in Turkey.

3. Kurdish Settlement Area and Kurdish Language

They do exist, though, the Kurds. Kurdistan comprises an area of 450,000 square kilometers surrounded by the settlement areas of the Persians, Azeri, Arabs, and Anatolian Turks. It is a mostly mountainous area with many forests, rich water resources, and numerous fertile plains. Agriculture has been at home here for thousands of years. It was here, that the Neolithic revolution began when the hunter-gatherers settled here and began farming the fields. The region is also called the cradle of civilization or passage area. Thanks to its geographical position, the Kurds have been able to protect their existence as an ethnic community until today. On the other hand, it was the exposed position of the Kurdish settlement area, which often wetted the appetite of external powers and invited raids and conquest. The Kurdish language reflects the influence of the Neolithic revolution, which is believed to have begun in the region of the Zagros and Taurus mountains. Kurdish belongs to the Indo-Germanic family of languages.

4. Outline of Kurdish History

It is highly probable that Kurdish language and culture began to develop during the fourth ice age (20,000 - 15,000 BC). The Kurds are one of the oldest autochthon populations in the region. About 6,000 BC they split into several branches. Historiography first mentions the Kurds as an ethnic group in connection with the Hurrites (3,000 – 2,000 BC). Therefore, it is assumed that the predecessors of the Kurds, the Hurrites, lived in tribal confederations and kingdoms together with the Mitanni, descendants of the Hurrites, the Nairi, the Urarteans, and the Medes. These political structures had already rudimentary state-like features. At that time, there were not yet any developed patriarchal social structures. In the Neolithic agricultural societies as well as in the Kurdish social structures women had a prominent position, which showed also in the Neolithic revolution.

It was Zoroastrism, which sustainably influenced and changed the Kurdish way of thinking in the time between 700 and 550 BC. Zoroastrism cultivated a way of life that was marked by work in the fields, where men and women were on par with each other. Love of animals had an important position and freedom was a high moral good. Zoroastrian culture equally influenced eastern and western civilization, since both Persians and Hellenes adopted many of its cultural influences. The Persian civilization, however, was founded by the Medes, which are believed to belong to the predecessors of the Kurds. In Herodotus' histories, there is much evidence for a division of power between both ethnic groups in the Persian Empire. This is also true for the subsequent Sassanid Empire.

During classic antiquity, the Hellenic era left deep traces in the eastern hemisphere. The principalities Abgar in Urfa and Komagene, the center of which was near Adiyaman-Samsat, and the kingdom of Palmyra in Syria were deeply influenced by the Greeks. We may say that it is there that we can find the first synthesis of oriental and occidental cultural influences. This special cultural encounter lasted until Palmyra was conquered by the Roman Empire in 269 AD, which brought about long-term negative consequences for the development of the entire region. The appearance of the Sassanid Empire also did not end the Kurdish influence. We may assume that during this time (216 – 652 AD) the feudal structures were formed in Kurdistan. With the rise of feudalism, the ethnic cohesion began to decay. The Kurdish society developed increasingly feudally structured bonds. This course of development towards a feudal civilization contributed sustainably to the Islamic revolution. Islam was directed against the slaveholder structures and changed the ethnical relations during the time of urbanization. At the same time, it revolutionized the feudal societies mentally and gave them an ideological basis.

The decline of the Sassanid Empire (650 AD) helped Islam create a feudal Kurdish aristocracy, which was strongly influenced by Arabic culture. It became one of the strongest social and political formations of its time. The Kurdish dynasty of the Eyyubi (1175 – 1250 AD) evolved into one of the most potent dynasties of the Middle East, exercising great influence on the Kurds.

On the other hand, the Kurds maintained close relations to the Seljuk sultanate, which took over the rule from the Abbasids in 1055. Dynasties of Kurdish descent like the Seddadis, Buyidis, and Marvanides (990 – 1090) developed into feudal petty states. Other principalities followed. The ruling class of the Kurds enjoyed a large autonomy in the Ottoman Empire.

In the 19th century, the Kurdish situation began to change dramatically. In the course of deteriorating relations with the Ottomans several Kurdish uprisings occurred. English and French missionaries brought the idea of separatism into the Armenian and Aramaic churches and thus contributed to a chaotic situation. Furthermore, the relations between Armenians, Assyrians and Kurds became notably worse. This fatal process ended in 1918 after World War II with the almost complete physical and cultural annihilation of the Armenians and Aramaeans, bearers of a culture several thousand years old.

Although the relations between Kurds and Turks had been seriously damaged, at the same time there was also a breach in the relations between the Kurds and the Armenians and Arameans.

5. Struggles for Resources – War and State Terror in Kurdistan

In the past, the geostrategic position of Kurdistan had wetted appetites, which had made the country a pawn in the struggles over the distribution of resources, wars, and state terror. This is still true today and goes back far into early history as Kurdistan had always been exposed to attacks and raids by external powers. The terror regimes of the Assyrian and Scythian Empires between 1000 and 1300 BC and the campaign of conquest by Alexander the Great are best-known examples. The Arab conquest was followed by the Islamization of Kurdistan. Much as Islam understands itself as a religion of peace, at its heart it has always been the warlike ideology of the Arab nation, which was able to spread quickly in Kurdistan. Islam proceeded into the foothills of the Taurus and Zagros mountains. Tribes that put up resistance were exterminated. In 1000 AD, Islam had hit its peak. Later, in the 13th and 14th centuries, the Mongols invaded Kurdistan. Flight and displacement followed. After the battle of Chaldoran in 1514, which saw the Ottomans come off as winners, the natural eastern border of the empire was shifted further eastward. The treaty of Qasr-e Shirin officially established the Iranian and Turkish borders and concluded the partition of Kurdistan, which has continued into the present. Mesopotamia and the Kurds found themselves for the most part within the borders of the Ottoman Empire. Until 1800, relative peace had prevailed between the Ottomans and the Kurdish principalities thanks to their shared Sunni Islamic belief. Alevitic and Zoroastrian Kurds, however, remained defiant and put up resistance in the mountains.

After 1800 until the decline of the Ottoman Empire, Kurdistan was shaken by numerous rebellions, which were usually bloodily crushed. After the end of the Ottomans, the Kurdish partition deepened even further, exacerbating the atmosphere of violence. The rising imperialist powers England and France redrew the boundaries in the Middle East, and Kurdistan was subjected to Turkish rule, the Iranian peacock throne, the Iraqi monarchy and the Syrian-French regime.

Under the impression of the loss of a large part of its former territories, Turkey switched over to a strict policy of assimilation in order to enforce the cohesion of the remaining parts of its former empire in this way. All indications of the existence of non- Turkish cultures in Turkey were to be exterminated. They even banned the use of the Kurdish language.

The aspiring Pahlavi dynasty in Iran proceeded in the same way. The rebellion of the Kurdish tribal leader Simko Shikak from Urmiye and the emancipation struggle of the Kurdish republic of Mahabad were crushed in blood. The Shah established a terror regime in the spirit of the nationalist-fascist epoch at the beginning of the 20th century. In the Iraqi and Syrian parts of Kurdistan, England and France suppressed the Kurdish emancipation efforts with the help of their Arab proxies. Here, too, a bloody colonial regime was established.

6. European Colonialism and the Kurdish Question

Driven by ambitions for geostrategic supremacy and boundless greed, the European intervention policy in the Middle East turned increasingly colonialist at the beginning of the 20th century. Its primary goal became the submission and control of the Middle East. This added a new form of colonialization to what the Kurds had already experienced over the course of history. The roots of this dilemma can be traced back to Sumerian times. Western capitalism, however, changed it in yet unimagined ways. Thus, the Kurds were again confronted with new colonialist actors. Resolving the Kurdish question had become even more difficult now.

With a view to their interests, the new imperialist powers deemed it more advantageous to seek cooperation with the sultan and the administration of the empire in order to win them as allies, instead of breaking up the Ottoman Empire with unforeseeable consequences. This approach aimed at alleviating control over the region and the people living there. This was a very popular method in the British Empire, which found its way into the history books as the "divide and rule" strategy. In this way, the Ottoman rule could be extended for another hundred years. France and Germany had similar strategies. Their frictions did not influence the balance of powers in the Middle East.

Yet another focus of the imperial preservation of power was put on the Christian ethnic groups. On the one hand, western colonialism pretended to protect the Anatolian Greeks, Armenians and Arameans; on the other hand, it encouraged these to revolt against the central power, which in turn responded by massive repression. The western powers watched the subsequent annihilation campaign with indifference. Eventually, this policy antagonized the nations of the Middle East to the imperialist powers. Again, the Kurds were only pawns in the game of foreign interests. In the past, the Kurdish aristocracy had collaborated with the Arab and Turkish dynasties. Now, they allowed foreign powers to use them for their colonialist intrigues. By winning the cooperation of the Kurds, the British succeeded to tie the anxious Turkish and Arab rulers to their own interests. Then again, they were able to tie the Armenians and Arameans further to the colonial powers, which in turn were hard-pressed by the Kurdish feudal collaborators. The Turkish sultan, the Persian shah and the Arab rulers were not only victims of this policy, though. The played a similar game in order to preserve their power and to curb the greediness of the western powers. The people suffered the consequences.

7. The Ideological Basis of Colonial Oppression and Power Politics in Kurdistan

Both the partition of Kurdistan and the forms of rule of the Arab, Persian, and Turkish regimes were a social setback for the Kurds in these parts of Kurdistan. Today's societal backwardness of the Kurds, which still stick to their feudal structures, is a product of these power relationships. With the coming of capitalist structures, from which the Kurds were mostly excluded anyway, the developmental divide between them and the Arab, Turkish, and Persian hegemonial societies grew larger. The power structures of the feudal rule mingled with bourgeois-capitalist power structures, which helped preserving the dominance of their corresponding nations. Although these structures depended on imperialism, they were able to build up their own national economies, further develop their own cultures, and stabilize their own state structures. In the areas of science and technology a national elite was coming of age. They forced all other ethnic groups in their countries to speak their language. With the help of a nationalist domestic and foreign policy, they created a national ruling class, which saw itself as a hegemonial power with a view to the other ethnic groups. Police and military were expanded and strengthened in order to break the resistance of the peoples. The Kurds were not able to respond to that. They still had to suffer from the impacts of the imperialist intrigues. They were confronted with the aggressive national chauvinism of the countries, which had the power in Kurdistan, and which explained the legitimacy of their power with adventurous ideological constructions.

7.1 Denial and Self-Denial

The hegemonial powers (i.e. Turkey, Iraq, Iran, and Syria) denied the Kurds their existence as an ethic group. In such surroundings, the Kurds ran a great risk when referring to themselves as Kurds publicly. Whenever they did so anyway, they could not even expect to be supported by their own ethnic group. For many Kurds their open commitment to their origin and culture resulted in exclusion from all economic and social relations. Therefore, many Kurds denied their ethnic descent or kept quiet about it, and the Middle Eastern regimes pushed this systematically. This denial strategy produced many absurdities. For the Arab Regimes the Kurdish question does not exist at all. They are certain that it must be and can be resolved by enforced Islamization. There is no other nation but Islam; and Islam is just another word for Arab.

The Persians even go a step farther and make the Kurds an ethnic subgroup of the Persians. In this way, the Kurds are granted all their rights in a natural way, or so they say. Kurds who demand their rights nonetheless and stick to their ethnic identity are regarded as people who throw mud at their own nation and who, therefore, must receive appropriate treatment.

The Turkish regime derives its claim for supremacy over the Kurds from alleged campaigns of conquest in Anatolia a thousand years ago. There had not been other ethnic groups there at that time they contend. Therefore, Kurd and Kurdistan are non-words, the corresponding people non-existent. Consequently, their existence cannot be recognized according to official ideology. The use of these non-words amounts to terrorist acts and needs to be punished accordingly.

However, in spite of all these ideological constructions: The Kurds are one of the oldest autochthon ethnic groups of the region.

7.2 Assimilation

Hegemonial powers often use the tool of assimilation when confronted with defiant ethnic groups. Language and culture are also potential carriers of resistance that can be desiccated by assimilation. Banning native languages and enforcing the use of a foreign language are quite effective tools. People, who are no longer allowed to speak their native language, will not be able to refer to the ethnic, geographic, and cultural characteristics they share through their mother tongue. Without speaking the same language, the amalgamating quality of collective ideas also disappears. Without this common basis, the web of interdependent relations within the ethnic group is broken down and dissolves. Consequently, the hegemonial language and culture gain ground in the conquered ethnic and language environment. The enforced use of the hegemonial language results in the withering of the native language until the latter becomes irrelevant. This happens even faster, when the native language, e.g. Kurdish, is not a literary language. Assimilation strategies are not restricted to the use of language. They can be applied in all public and social areas controlled by the state.

Kurdistan has often been the stage for cultural assimilation attempts by foreign hegemonial powers. The past hundred years of its history, however, have been the most destructive. The creation of modern nation-state structures in the hegemonial countries and the creation of a colonial system of rule in Kurdistan aggravated the assimilation attempts directed at the Kurdish language and culture. Like Persian and Arabic in the past, Turkish now became the hegemonial language by force. While the Kurds had been able to preserve their culture and language during antiquity and middle ages, now the three hegemonial languages and cultures took over. They also had the whole set of modern media and communication tools at their disposal. Kurdish traditional songs and literature were banned. Thus, the Kurdish language, which had produced many works of literature in the antiquity, was suddenly threatened in its existence. Kurdish culture and language were declared subversive elements. Native language education was banned. The hegemonial languages became the only languages that were allowed in the educational system, and thus the only languages used to teach the achievements of modernity.

The Turkish, Persian, and Arab nation-states pursued a systematic assimilation policy using a variety of repressive means both institutionally and socially, all of which purposefully denied the Kurdish language and culture any legitimacy. Only the language and culture of the hegemony were meant to stay alive.

7.3 Religion and Nationalism

The hegemony also uses religion and nationalism to preserve its supremacy. In all parts of Kurdistan Islam is state religion and used by the hegemonial powers to exercise control over the population. Even if these regimes verbally embrace secularism, the entanglement of political and religious institutions is obvious. While there is an openly theocratic regime in Iran, other countries try to conceal the political instrumentalization of religion. Therefore, the Turkish national religious authority employs several hundred thousand Imams. Even Iran does not possess such an army of religious leaders. The religious schools in Turkey are under the direct control of the state.

Koran schools and theological institutes and faculties employ almost half a million people. This makes the constitutional postulate of secularism look absurd and rather appear like a placebo.

Wherever these ideas hit upon political reality, the situations turns chaotic. Under the DP (Democracy Party) and the AP (Justice Party) governments, religion was politicized openly. The military coups in March 1971 and September 1980 modified the Turkish ideological framework and redefined the role of religion. This initiated the re-islamization of the Turkish republic, similar to what had happened in Iran after Khomeini had seized power in 1979, albeit not that radical. In 2003, the AKP (Justice and Development Party) came into power and with it, for the first time,

Islamic ideologues became part of the government. This election victory was no accident but the result of the long-term religious policy of the Turkish state.

7.4 Middle-Class Nationalism

Another ideological tool of the hegemonial powers is the nationalism of the middle class. This ideology had developed in the 19th and 20th centuries when it became the dominant ideology of the nation-states. It formed the basis for the middle class to proceed against the interests of the workers and the real-socialist tendencies. Eventually, nationalism emerged as a logical result of the nation-state that was attributed almost religious features.

The Turkish form of nationalism that came into being after 1840 was an attempt to prevent the decay of the Ottoman Empire that had begun to show. The early Turkish nationalists were originally Ottoman legalists. Only later they turned against the sultanate of Abdulhamid II and became increasingly radical. The nationalism of the Young Turk movement expressed itself in the committee for unity and progress, which worked for a constitutional reform of the state and aspired towards power in the empire. Apart from that, they had always made it clear that they wanted to strengthen the empire again. Since the empire had become weak externally and was threatened by internal decay, they wanted to systematically modernize its political, military, and economical foundations. Subsequently, the German foreign policy offensive in the Middle East and Central Asia added a racist component to Turkish nationalism. The genocide of the Armenians, Pontic Greeks, Aramaeans, and Kurds followed. The young Turkish republic was marked by aggressive nationalism and a very strict conception of the nation-state. The slogan "one language, one nation, one country" became its political dogma. Although this approach was essentially classless and fraternal, the instruments to actually implement it were simply not available. Its abstractness bore the danger of ideological fanaticism. Nationalism thus degraded into a tool for the ruling circles that used it to cover up their failures. Under the flag of "superior Turkish identity" the entire society was sworn to an aggressive nationalism.

The war in Kurdistan and the terrorism of the state created a separate power bloc. This power bloc, similar to power blocs in other systems, derived its power from the military and based its existence on continued war in such a way that the society mirrored its structures.

This is also, why the political system lost its ability to solve conflicts. This system had been formed by war and state terror. It remained unclear, which power centers served which interests and goals, a fact with equally disastrous effects for both Turkish and Kurdish communities.

8. Kurdish Identity and Kurdish Resistance

The Kurds started only comparatively late to form a national identity of their own. Even if there was some awareness of a shared identity in the Kurdish rebellions of the 19th century, it did not go beyond forming a combined opposition against the sultanate and the rule of the shah. There were no concepts for alternative ways of life. Any commitment to the Kurdish national identity involved the wish to create a Kurdish kingdom similar to the medieval sultanates. For a long time, the Kurds were very far away from identifying themselves as a nation. It was only in the second half of the 20th century that the idea of a Kurdish identity began to emerge from intellectual debates largely on the Turkish left. However, this trend lacked the intellectual potential to overcome the more traditional understanding of Kurdish identity, which rested on the tribal order and the sheikdom. Both the real-socialist communist parties as well as the liberal and feudal parties were still far from understanding the idea of a Kurdish nation or the idea of the Kurds as an ethnic group. Only the leftist student movement of the 1970s was able to contribute substantially to the awareness of a Kurdish identity.

The ethnic identification process developed in the conflict between Turkish chauvinist national understanding and Kurdish feudal national understanding. On the one hand, there was the confrontation with the ideological hegemony of the system, often enough dresses in leftist phrases, on the other hand there was the confrontation with the Kurdish aristocracy, who traditionally cooperated with the system. Liberation from these societal, political, and ideological forces did not come easy. It required both intellectual potential and practical organizational work. This way, however, led directly into resistance. Since the 1970s, when the Kurdish emancipation efforts had not yet come of age, thirty-five years have passed. This time did not only enlighten the Kurds over their own identity and suggest approaches for a solution of the Kurdish question; it also shows that the Kurds and their emancipation cannot be forcibly suppressed in the long run, and that the obvious social contradictions cannot be forcibly transformed. The Kurdish emancipation struggle also demonstrates that the people cannot develop without winning back the dignity of the society.

9. The Kurdistan Workers Party (PKK)

9.1 History and Origins of the PKK

In April 1973 a group of six people came together in order to form an independent Kurdish political organization. They acted on the assumption that Kurdistan was a classic colony, where the population was forcibly refused the right to self-determination. It was their key goal to change this. This gathering was the hour of birth of a new Kurdish movement.

Over the years, this group found new followers who helped spread the message among the rural population of Kurdistan. More and more often, they were involved in clashes with Turkish security forces, armed tribesmen of the Kurdish aristocracy, or rival political groups violently attacking the young movement. On 27 November 1978, the Kurdistan Workers Party (PKK) was founded in a small village near Diyarbakir. Twenty-two leading members of the movement took part in the foundational meeting in order to give the movement more professional structures. In an urban environment, the movement would not have survived, so they focused their activities on the rural Kurdish regions.

The Turkish authorities reacted harshly to the propaganda efforts of the PKK. Detentions and armed clashes followed. Both sides experienced losses. The overall situation in Turkey, however, was also heating up. The first signs of the imminent military coup were already visible in 1979. The PKK responded by withdrawing from Turkey into the mountains or into other countries of the Middle East. Only a small number of activists remained in Turkey. This step helped the PKK to secure their survival. On September 12, 1980, the Turkish military overthrew the civil government and seized power. The military junta then imprisoned many of the PKK who had remained in Turkey.

In this situation, the PKK had to determine, whether they wanted to become an exile organization or a modern national liberation movement. After a short phase of re-organization, a majority of members returned to Kurdistan and resumed the armed resistance against the fascist junta. The attacks on military facilities in Eruh and Semdili on August 15, 1984 proclaimed the official beginning of the armed resistance. Although there were still some deficits, the move towards organizing a national liberation movement had been made.

Originally, the Turkish authorities - Turgut Ozal had just been elected prime minister – tried to play down the incidents. The national propaganda called the guerilla a "handful of bandits", which was quite revealing about the mindset of the responsible politicians in Ankara. A political approach to the conflict was not visible. By and by, the clashes grew into outright war, which demanded numerous victims on both sides.

It was only in the 1990s, that the situation became less gridlocked, when the state seemed to become ready for a political solution. Some statements by Turgut Ozal and Suleyman Demirel, then president, seemed to indicate that they might be ready to recognize the Kurdish identity. This raised hopes for an early end of the conflict. The PKK tried to strengthen this process by declaring a ceasefire in 1993. Turgut Ozal's sudden death, however removed one of the most important figures for this process from the board. Other obstacles came up. Some hardliners among the PKK wanted to continue the armed struggle; the situation in the leadership of the Turkish state was difficult and marked by conflicting interests; the attitude of the Iraqi Kurdish leaders Talabani and Barzani was also not helpful in deepening the peace process. It had been the biggest opportunity for a peaceful solution of the Kurdish question until then, and it was lost.

Subsequently the conflict escalated again. Both parties experienced high losses. However, even this escalation did not lift the deadlock. The years of war between 1994 and 1998 were lost years. In spite of several unilateral ceasefires on the part of the PKK, the Turkish state insisted on a military solution. The ceasefire of 1998 remained without response as well. Rather, it stirred up a military confrontation between Turkey and Syria, which brought both countries to the edge of a war. In 1998, I went to Europe as chairman of the PKK in order to promote a political solution. The following odyssey is well known. I was abducted from Kenya in violation of international law and brought to Turkey. This abduction was backed by an alliance of secret services and the public expected the conflict to escalate then. However, the trial on the Turkish prison island of Imrali marked a political U-turn in the conflict and offered new perspectives for a political solution. At the same time, this turn caused the PKK to reconsider its ideological and political orientation. I had already been working on these points before my abduction, real ideological and political turning point. Thus, what had been the real motives?

9.2. Main Criticisms

Doubtlessly, my abduction was a heavy blow for the PKK. It was nonetheless not the reason for the following ideological and political cut. Originally, the PKK had been conceived as a party with state-like hierarchical structures similar to other parties. Such structures, however, are in dialectical contrast to the principles of democracy, freedom, and equality, a contradiction in principle concerning political parties in general regardless of their particular philosophy. Although the PKK fought for the cause of freedom, we had not been able to free ourselves from thinking in hierarchical structures.

Another main contradiction was the PKK's quest for institutional political power, which correspondingly formed and aligned the party. Structures aligned along the lines of institutional power, however, are in conflict with societal democratization, which the PKK had declared to be fighting for. Activists of traditional parties tend to orient themselves towards their superiors rather than towards the general society, or as the case may be, aspire to superior positions themselves. All of the three big ideological tendencies based on emancipative social conceptions are confronted with this contradiction. Real-socialism and social democracy as well as national liberation movements when trying to implement social conceptions beyond capitalism cannot free themselves from the ideological constraints of the capitalist system. Thus, they became pillars of the capitalist system quite early in pursuing institutional political power instead of focusing on the democratization of the society.

Another main contradiction was the value given to war in the ideological and political considerations of the PKK. War was understood as the continuation of politics by different means and romanticized as a strategic instrument.

This was a blatant contradiction to our self-perception as a movement struggling for the liberation of the society. According to this, the use of armed force can only be justified for the purpose of necessary self-defense. Anything going beyond that would be in violation of the socially emancipative approach that the PKK felt itself obliged to, since it had always been the repressive regimes in history that had relied on war or had aligned their institutions according to the logic of warfare. The PKK had believed that leading an armed struggle for the Kurdish rights was sufficient. Such a deterministic idea of war is neither socialist nor democratic, although the PKK saw itself as a democratic party. A truly socialist party does not rely on state structures and hierarchies or structure itself according to state structures. It does not aspire to institutional political power, since the basis of institutional power is the protection of particular interests and the preservation of power by means of war.

The putative defeat of the PKK allegedly accomplished by my abduction to Turkey, was eventually reason enough to critically and openly look into the reasons that had prevented our liberation movement from making better progress. The ideological and political cut after that undergone by the PKK, made the putative defeat a departure to new horizons.

10. New Approaches of the Kurdish Liberation Movement

In this essay, I cannot accomplish a comprehensive treatment of the main strategic, ideological, philosophical, and political elements underlying the process of change.

However, its cornerstones are the following:

• The philosophical, political and value-related approaches that the re-aligned PKK embraces find their adequate expression in the term "democratic socialism".

• The PKK does not derive the creation of a Kurdish nation-state from the right of peoples to self-determination. However, we regard this right as a basic right for the establishment of grassroots democracy, without seeking to establish new political borders. It is up to the PKK to convince the Kurdish society of this approach. The same is also true for talks with the hegemonial countries exercising power in Kurdistan. They will be the basis for a resolution of the existing issues.

• The existing countries need real democratic reforms going beyond mere lip service to democracy. It is not realistic, though, to demand the immediate abolition of the state. However, I do not mean to say that we have to take it as it is. The classical state structure with its despotic attitude to power is unacceptable. The institutional state needs to undergo democratic changes. At the end of this process, the state should be a lean political institution with functions limited to internal and external security, and the provision of social security. Such an understanding of the state has nothing in common with the authoritarian character of the classical state. Rather it would resemble a societal authority.

• The Kurdish liberation movement is working for a system of democratic self-organization in Kurdistan with the features of a confederation. The term democratic confederalism describes a coordination model for a democratic nation. It provides a framework, within which minorities, religious communities, cultural groups, gender-specific groups and other societal groups can organize themselves autonomously. We may call this model "organizational framework for democratic nations and civilizations". The democratization process in Kurdistan is not limited to matters of form but, rather, constitutes a broad societal project aiming at the economic, social, and political sovereignty of all parts of the society. It advances the buildup of necessary institutions and creates the instruments for democratic self-government and control. It is devised as a continuous long-term process. Elections are not the only democratic tool in this context. Rather, we view this process as a dynamic one, which needs direct intervention by the sovereign people. The people are to be directly involved in the decision-finding processes of the society. This project relies on the self-government of local communities and is organized in the form of open councils, town councils, local parliaments, and larger congresses. Citizens themselves are the agents of this kind of self-government instead of state-based institutions. The principle of federative self-government has no limitations. It can even be continued across borders in order to create multinational democratic structures. Democratic confederalism prefers flat hierarchies where decision finding and decision making processes take place within local communities.

• The model outlined above may be described as autonomous democratic self-government with limited sovereign rights of the state. Other than traditional administrative models, this model allows for a more adequate implementation of basic values like freedom and equality. This model is also applicable in the other parts of Kurdistan. At the same time, it is suitable for the buildup of federative administrative structures in all Kurdish settlement areas in Syria, Turkey, Iraq and Iran. Thus, it is possible to build confederate structures across all parts of Kurdistan without the need to question the existing borders.

• The decline of real-socialism was also a result of the way socialist countries used their power internally and externally, and in the fact that they misconceived the importance of the gender issue. Women and power are categories very much in mutual contradiction. In real-socialism, the question of women's rights was a rather subordinate issue, which would be resolved once the economic and other societal problems were resolved. However, we should rather regard women as an oppressed class, nation instead of just as the oppressed gender. As long as we do not discuss freedom and equal treatment of women in a historical and societal context, as long as we have no adequate theory for this, our practice will not be adequate either. Therefore, women's liberation must assume a main strategic position in the democratic struggle for freedom in Kurdistan.

• The democratization of politics is one of our urgent challenges today. However, democratic politics needs democratic parties. As long as there are no parties and party-affiliated institutions committed to the interests of the society instead of fulfilling state orders, a democratization of politics will be hardly possible. In Turkey, the parties are only propaganda tools of the state enjoying public alimentation. Their transformation into true parties committed exclusively to the interests of the society, and the creation of the necessary legal basis for this, would be an important part of any political reform. The founding of parties bearing the word Kurdistan in their name is still a criminal act. Independent parties are still obstructed in many ways. Kurdistan-related parties or coalitions in fact serve democratization as long as they do not become advocates of separatism or violence.

• There is a widespread individual and institutional subservient spirit, which is one of the biggest obstacles for democratization. It can only be overcome be creating an awareness for democracy in all parts of the society. Citizens need to be invited to commit themselves to democracy. For the Kurds, this entails the build of democratic structures in all parts of Kurdistan to advance the active participation of the Kurds in the political life of the community. Minorities living in Kurdistan must be invited to participate as well. The development of grassroots-level democratic structures and a corresponding practical approach must have top priority. Such grassroots structures have to be regarded as mandatory even in places where basic democratic and legal principles are violated such as the Middle East.

• Politics needs independent media. Without them, the structures of the state will not develop any sensitivity for questions of democracy. Nor will it be possible to bring democracy into politics. Freedom of information is not only a right of the individual. It also involves a societal dimension. Independent media have also always a societal mandate. Their communication with the public must be determined by democratic balance.

• Feudal relics like tribes, sheiks, aghas, and sectarians, which are essentially relics of the Middle Ages, are obstacles in the way of democratization like the institutions of classic nation-states. They must be pressed adequately to join the democratic change. It must become a top priority to overcome these parasitic institutions.

• The right to native language education must be guaranteed. Even if the authorities do not advance such education, they must not impede civic efforts for the creation of institutions offering Kurdish language and culture education. The existence of the health system must be guaranteed by both state and civil society.

• Ecological models of the society are essentially socialist models. The establishment of an ecological balance can only be accomplished during the transition from an alienated class society based on despotism to a socialist society. It would be an illusion to hope for the conservation of the environment in a capitalist system. These systems largely participate in the ecological devastation. Protection of the environment must be given broad consideration in the process of societal change.

• The solution of the Kurdish question will be found within the framework of the democratization of the countries exercising hegemonial power over the different parts of Kurdistan. This process is not limited to these countries, though, but rather extends across the entire Middle East. The freedom of Kurdistan is tied to the democratization of the Middle East. A free Kurdistan is only conceivable as a democratic Kurdistan.

• The individual rights to freedom of expression and the freedom of choice are indispensable. No country, no state, no society has the right to restrict these freedoms, for any reason whatsoever.

Without the freedom of the individual, there will be no freedom for the society, just as freedom for the individual is impossible when the society is not free.

• A just redistribution of the economic resources, which are presently in the possession of the state, is highly important for the liberation of the society. Economic supply must not be used to put pressure on the people with the help of the state. The economic resources are the property of the society and not the property of the state.

• An economy close to the people should be based on just redistribution and be for the benefit of the people instead of pursuing exclusively the accumulation and increase of surplus value and turnover. The local economical structures do not only damage the society but also the environment. One of the main reasons for the decline of the society lies in the effects of the local finance markets. The artificial production of needs, the more and more adventurous search for new sales markets and the endless greed for even bigger profits allows the existing divide between rich and poor to grow steadily and enlarges the army of people living below the poverty line or even dying of hunger. An economic policy like this cannot be tolerated anymore. The biggest challenge for a socialist policy thus is the implementation of an alternative economic policy, which is not exclusively guided by profit but rather by the just distribution of resources and the satisfaction of natural needs.

• Although the Kurds highly value their families, they are still places where freedom does not exactly abound. Lack of financial resources, lack of education, lack of health care do not allow for much development. The situation of women and children is disastrous. So-called honor-killings of female family members are characteristic of this disaster. They become targets of an archaic notion of honor, which reflects the degeneration of the entire society. Male frustration over the existing conditions is directed against women, supposedly the weakest members of the society. The family as a social institution experiences a crisis. Here, too, a solution can only be found in the context of a general democratization of the society.

11. Present Situation and Possible Solutions

The Kurdish-Turkish relations in Turkey play a key role for a solution of the Kurdish question whereas the Kurds of Iraq, Iran, and Syria have only a limited potential and can probably only contribute some support to a possible overall solution. The Kurds in Iraq pose a very good example. The semi-state Kurdish autonomy is the indirect result of worldwide efforts on the part of Turkey, the U.S. and their allies to denounce the PKK as a terror organization. Without consent by Ankara, this "solution" would not have been possible. The chaos caused by it is obvious, and the future unforeseeable. It is also unclear, which direction the feudal-liberal Kurdish national authority in Iraq will take in the long run and how it will affect Iran, Syria, and Turkey. There is the danger that the conflict might escalate and become similar to the Israeli-Palestinian conflict. A flare-up of Kurdish nationalism might radicalize the Persian, Arab and Turkish nationalists further, making a solution of the problem even more difficult.

This prospect needs to be contrasted with a solution free of nationalist aspirations, which recognizes the existing territorial borders. In return, the status of the Kurds will have to be included in the respective constitutions in order to guarantee and safeguard their cultural and language rights and their political participation. Such a model would largely be in accordance with the historical and societal realities of the region.

This said, making peace with the Kurds seems inevitable as it seems highly improbable that the present as well as any future war will produce anything else but a Pyrrhus' victory. Therefore, this war must be ended. It has already lasted too long. It is in the interest of all countries of the region to follow the example of other countries and take the necessary steps.

The Kurds only demand respect for their existence; they demand freedom of culture and a fully democratic system. A more humane and modest solution is impossible. The examples of South Africa, Palestine, Wales, Northern Ireland, Scotland, and Corsica demonstrate the ways in which different modern countries have been able to solve similar problems in the course of their history. Furthermore, these comparisons help us to find a more objective approach to our own problems.

Renunciation of violence as a means to solve the Kurdish question and overcoming the repressive policy of denial at least in part depend upon the continued existence of a democratic option. The ban on Kurdish language and culture education and broadcasting is in itself a terrorist act and practically invites counter violence. Violence, however, has been used by both sides to an extent that goes clearly beyond legitimate self defense.

Many movements today have used even more extreme methods. We, however, have declared several unilateral ceasefires. We have withdrawn large numbers of our fighters from Turkish territory disproving the accusation of terrorism. Our peace efforts, however, have always been ignored. Our initiatives have never met a response. On the contrary, when a group of Kurdish politicians was sent out as ambassadors of peace, they were detained and handed long prison terms. Our efforts for peace have been interpreted as weakness. This is wrong. There is no other explanation for statements that described the PKK and Ocalan as practically finished and called our initiatives only tactical. Therefore, they claimed, they only needed to proceed a little bit tougher in order to smash the PKK. Therefore, they increased their attacks on the Kurdish liberation movement. Nobody asks, however, why they never succeeded? It is impossible to solve the Kurdish question by means of violence. The attitude described above also contributed to the failure of the ceasefire that began on October 1, 2006. I had called on the PKK to offer this ceasefire. Some intellectuals and non-government organizations had demanded such a step. However, again they did not take it seriously. Instead, racism and chauvinism were stirred up and created an atmosphere of confrontation. Besides, we must not forget that the AKP also uses the Kurdish issue to play down their own problems with the Kemalist elite by making compromises with the Army and speculating on the escalation of the Kurdish problem. Presently, the government restricts itself to some half-hearted measures in order to wrench some concessions from the EU. They are trying to win time with the help of the harmonization laws enacted in the context of the EU accession process. In reality, these supposed reforms are just waste paper.

The exacerbation of the conflict is in fact cause for concern. Nevertheless, I will not give up my hopes for a just peace. It can become possible at any time.

I offer the Turkish society a simple solution. We demand a democratic nation. We are not opposed to the unitary state and republic. We accept the republic, its unitary structure and laicism. However, we believe, that it must be redefined as a democratic state respecting peoples, cultures and civil rights. On this basis, the Kurds must be free to organize themselves democratically and unfold their culture, language, economy and ecology. This would allow Kurds, Turks, and other cultures to come together under the roof of a Democratic Nation of Turkey. This is only possible, though, with a democratic constitution, a democratic understanding of the idea of a nation and an advanced multicultural system of law.

Our idea of a democratic nation is not defined by flags and borders. Our idea of a democratic nation embraces a model based on democracy instead of a model based on state structures and ethnic origins. Turkey as a nation must embrace all its ethnic groups. This would entail the concept of a nation, which is based on human rights instead of religion or race or Turkish ethnicity. Our idea of a democratic nation includes all ethnic groups and cultures.

Against this backdrop let me once more summarize the cornerstones of a possible solution:

• The Kurdish question must be treated as a fundamental question of democratization. The Kurdish identity must be put down in the constitution and integrated in the legal system. This demand would be fulfilled if the new constitution contained an article of the following wording: "The constitution of the Turkish republic recognizes the existence and the expression of all its cultures in a democratic way." This would be sufficient.

• Cultural and language rights must be protected by law. There must not be any restrictions for radio, TV, and press. Kurdish programs and programs in other languages must be treated by the same rules and regulations that are applied to Turkish programs. The same must also be true for cultural activities.

• Kurdish language should be taught in elementary schools. People, who want their kids to get such an education, must be able to send them to such a school. High schools should offer lessons on Kurdish culture, language, and literature as elective courses. Universities must be permitted to establish institutes for Kurdish language, literature, culture, and history.

• Freedom of expression and freedom of association must not be restricted. The state must not restrict or regulate political This also holds without restrictions for activities in the context of the Kurdish question.

• Party and election laws must be reformed democratically. The law must provide for the participation of the Kurdish people and all other democratic groups in the processes of democratic decision-making.

• Municipal administrations must be put on a legal basis, which strengthens democracy.

• The village-guard system and the illegal networks within the state-structures must be disbanded.

• People forcibly evicted from their villages during the war must be able to return without obstructions . All administrative, legal, economical, or social measures necessary to ensure their return must be met. Furthermore, developmental programs must be set up that help the Kurdish population to earn a living and improve their standard of living.

• A law for peace and participation in the society shall be enacted. This law shall create the legal basis for the members of the guerilla, the imprisoned, and those who are in exile, to take part in the democratic political life without any preconditions.

Additionally, immediate measures on the road to a solution need to be discussed. A democratic action plan must be formulated and got underway. In order to reconcile the society, truth and justice commissions shall be set up. Both sides must lay open their past wrongs truthfully. This is the only way to achieve the reconciliation of the society.

Whenever countries or organizations have reached a dead end, intellectuals may serve as mediators. South Africa, Northern Ireland, or Sierra Leone have made positive experiences with this model. They may take the role of arbitrators, who can move both parties in the direction of a just peace. Such commissions may include intellectuals, lawyers, physicians, or scientists. When some day we will lay down our arms, we will only hand our arms over to such a commission, provided this commission is determined to achieve justice.

Why would we surrender our arms without the prospect of justice? The beginning of such a process also depends on goodwill and the existence of a dialogue. Should there be a dialogue, we will be able to begin a process similar to the last unlimited ceasefire.

I am prepared to do all I can. The government, however, needs to show its will for peace. It needs to take the initiative. Otherwise, the government alone will be held accountable for the consequences.

In case our efforts for a peaceful solution should fail or be sacrificed to the politics of the day, or some power struggle or profit seeking, the present conflict will exacerbate and its outcome become unforeseeable. In the chaos that follows there will be no winners.

At last, Turkey needs to muster the strength to recognize its own reality, the reality of the Kurdish existence and the global dynamics. A country, which denies reality, will inevitably slip into an existential crisis eventually.

It is crucial, therefore, to take the steps that will lead this country to a lasting peace.

Abdullah Ocalan, Imrali Prison